Scent of Crushed Petals

An Anthology of short poems

Scent of Crushed Petals

An Anthology of short poems

Poems by

MADHU BHAGAT

Wordly Wise Publishers

Published by
Wordly Wise Publishers
39-A, JMD Building, Rajpur Khurd,
Chattarpur, New Delhi 110068
+91-9836325999
hello@wordlywise.co.in
www.wordlywise.co.in

First Published in 2022

ISBN: 978-93-94075-06-1

A few lines which really moved me

'I walked a mile with Pleasure
She chatted all the way,
But left me none the wiser
For all she had fo say.

I walked a mile with Sorrow
And ne'er a word said she,
But,oh!the things I learnt form her
When Sorrow walked with me

By
Robert Browning Hamilton

Dedicated
To
The Universe ...for giving me
this inspiration to create

To
My Dearest Parents
Kushal Chand & Kamesh Kanta Suri

To
My Beloved husband
Wg Cdr.Narinder Kumar Bhagat
Miss you

Acknowledgment

Heartfelt & Loving thanks to my
Beautiful daughters
Sunaina Bhagat
Shefali Bhagat
And loving son
Vaarun Bhagat
For always giving me their unstinting support
Believing in me &
For Standing by my side at all times
Loving thanks to my son-in-law(more than a son)
Vikas Rana
For his constant and consistent words of
encouragement
Soulful thanks and Blessings
To my Adorable Grandchildren-
Sanna
Aishwarya & Adheraj
For their unconditional Love and adulation

Heartfelt & Grateful thanks to my elder sister
Kowkab Jabeen Nasir-
For giving me strength and being by my side
always.

To my loving brothers Sunil Suri,Anil Suri &
my younger sister Reena.
And
My (late) elder Brother Narotam Kumar Suri

Special Thanks

And Lots of Love
To my 14 year old Angel
Tejal Kaur Ghandhoke
Without her love and encouragement
I couldn't have compiled my book.

Heartfelt thanks to the
Very talented Rugwed Rajesh Jadhav
For completely understanding every written and unwritten word
And making the timeless Illustrations.

Grateful thanks dear Sahil Bhambri and Chandni Mathur for helping me put this book together in such a short time.

Loving thanks
To my beautiful selfless soulmate
For being by my side,
Dr Meena Bajaj

Preface

It is said that everyone has two lives:

The second one starts when you realise you only have one!!

I am taking this opportunity,

which God has given me,to put my thoughts into words

The baring of my heart

The baring of my soul

Clear and Translucent

I hope I am able to convey my every emotion to my reader.

Poems are a concised version of the larger than life stories

When we pen our thoughts

We bare our souls

May every word stir your Heart as it has my Being

Contents

1.	The Sound Of Time - Passing You By	18
2.	Moments	22
3.	Woven Weaves	26
4.	A Bond Unfathomable	30
5.	The Truth	34
6.	The Erroneous Era	38
7.	In Pursuit of Happiness	42
8.	The Global Woman: Wither is she Bound?	46
9.	And I Walked	50
10.	A Painful Existence	54
11.	A Cotton Seed	58
12.	Alone—In the Market Place	62
13.	A Twinkling Star—A Juvenile in Jeopardy	68
14.	A Silent Ode	72
15.	Eternity Moment	76
16.	The Awakening	80
17.	Silence	84
18.	Life	88
19.	Your Essence, Your Soul	92
20.	When Time Stands Still	96
21.	The Lingering Cessation The Wait	100
22.	The Hazy Picture	104
23.	The Tumultuous Turbulence	108

In a world of material artefacts

Words are an intangible treasure.

The Sound Of Time - Passing You By

Have you heard
The tinkle of seconds?
Have you smelt
The fragrance of minutes?
Have you felt
The touch of hours?
Have you seen
The passage of years?

Have you tasted
The flavour of time?

Have you heard the sound
Of time passing you by?

On a richter scale
Or a barometer
Have you measured the tremors of joy
And weighed the whimper of sorrows?

The heights and the strides
Of loneliness
Have you felt the weight
Of an unshed tear?
Have you tasted the salt of a wayward drop
Moist on your lips,
An olfactory experience?

A brush of thc hand
A flicker of the eyelid
A twist of the shoulder

The passing of seasons
The heightened senses
Behold
The sound of time passing you by

A poet is a philosopher
Who finds meaning in madness.

Moments

Intangible yet substantial
Life is moments
A collection
A compilation of moments
Happy moments, sad moments

Hilarious, exhilarating
and ecstatic moments
Bleak and depressing moments

Moment: A spilt second
An atom of
Joy or sorrow

Displaying the end
Or the beginning of another
moment

A moment is what is yours
Keep it alive

Covert and prance
Enjoy it
Accept it, feel it
Imbibe it within yourself
Live it

For life is moments

A collection...
A herd, a cluster, a clump
A flock, a bunch, a swarm
Of moments

Precious and precocious
Defined and redefined

Intangible yet substantial
Moments

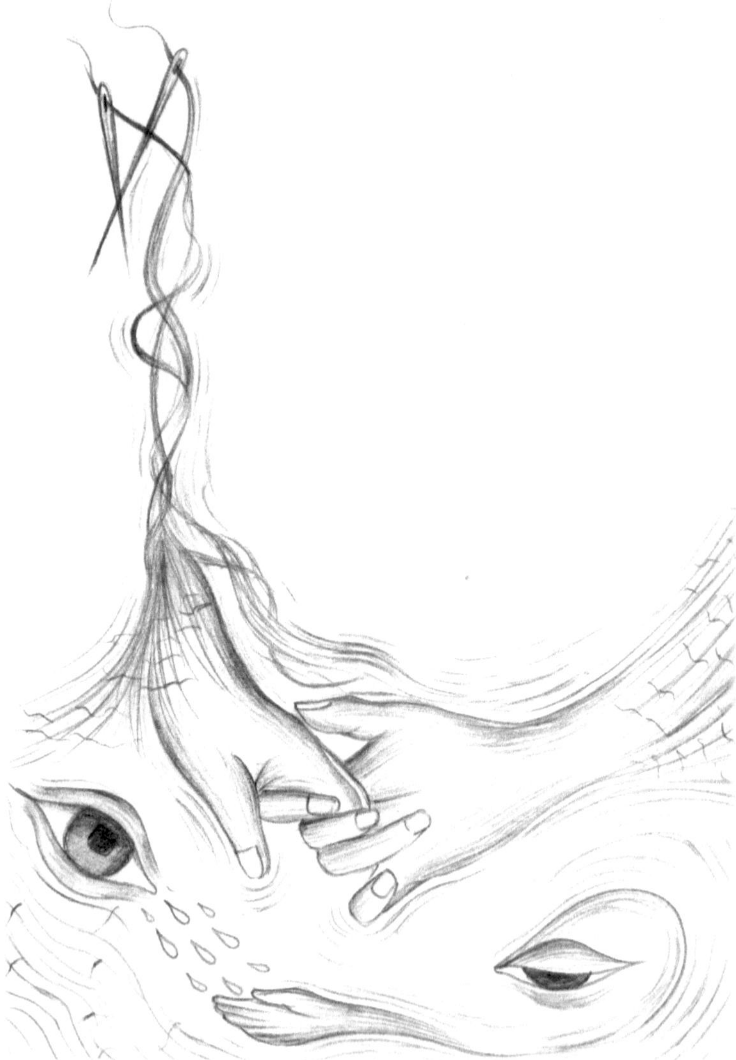

A philosopher is a poet
Who finds madness in meaning.

Woven Weaves

Woven weaves when winnowed
Lie naked and threadbare
Woven weaves when winnowed
Have always a tale to share

Come sit with me a moment high
You'll hear, feel and see
The strength, with which the weaves were woven
No thread would ever be free

Now the sifting tells anew
The warped tale 'tis but for few
The shine, the Sheen
Shone wondrously
Of the silken threads entwined
As the luminous warp
And the lustrous woof lay woven
A fabric wove so fine

An unwritten statute
An unspoken ordinance
Wove and interwove a tale
A breathless wonder unfolded
A divinity born
A magnetic chemistry
Wove the silken yarn!

The woven weaves
Were you and me
A historic sight for all to see
Once a timeless wonder

Now on the hearth
The mauled remains
Lay tangled and threadbare
For once the woven weaves are winnowed
There's always a tale to share

When we pen our thoughts
We bare our souls and
Unclothe our inner self.

A Bond Unfathomable

Mother, a synonym
A pillar invincible, indomitable
An idol of endurance, a mountain
A guru of perseverance; a stupa

An indestructible spirit, immortal

Many a volcano has she survived
Many an earthquake has she weathered
Thru' tornadoes she has stood her ground; unshaken
Thru floods she has swum, struggled and surfaced.

A torch in hand, she leads her brood
A leader of leaders
Strong as the westerly winds yet soft as a Lily
Ramrod straight her stem remains
Yet pliable like the soft earth
Which bends, 'n' twists' 'n' turns'
To feed and clothe her young ones

She moulds them, she prepares them
As a potter moulds his wares
She cocoons them in her ample bosom
A tigress in sheep's clothing
Ready to claw and kill

A bond: a gift of divinity
The umbilical cord
Though scissored at birth
Never actually severed

She carries her childrens'
 heart in her own
As she carried them in her womb

A bond…unfathomable

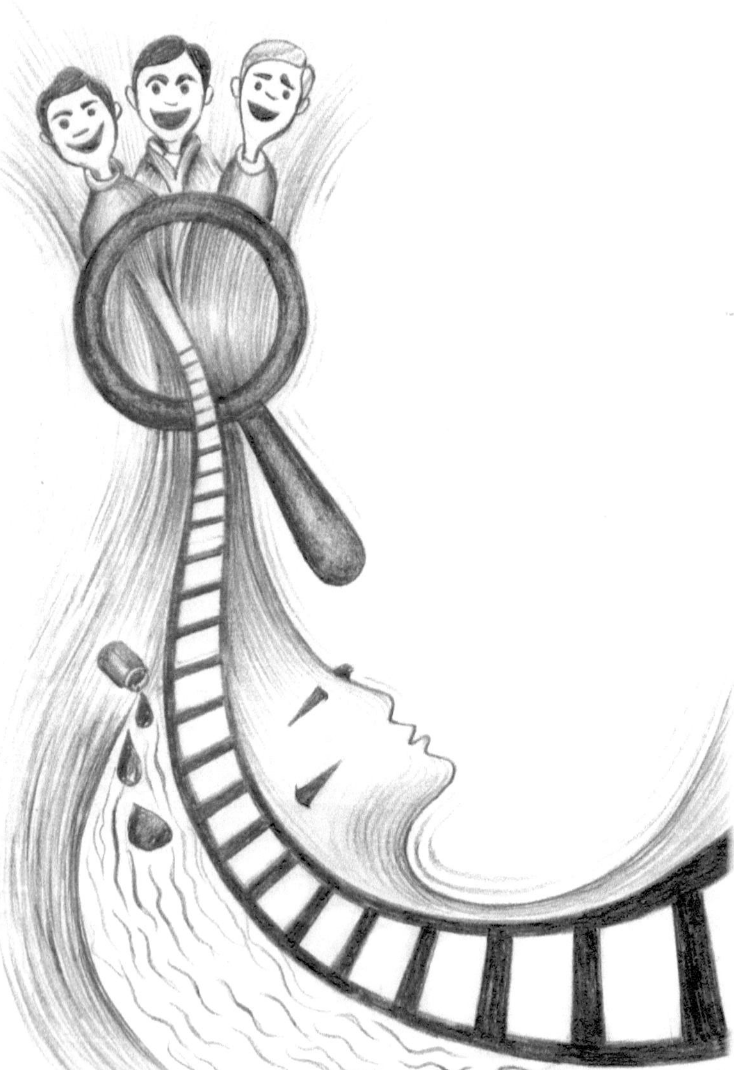

In an era of meaningless misers
There are many who silently
Give a loud whisper of
encouragement.

The Truth

A quest, a search, a hunt,
Unravel the mysteries,
Seek the truth...for to live
A life of lie, is but a life half lived

Prepare the armour
Don the nerves of steel
For you to brave the piercing arrow
Tipped with poison...Lest it pinions and slays
The pulsating dove within your bosom

Truth is painful, bear it
Hear it, feel it
Hark! It is where the angels live
Near God, nigh providence

Your journey, though long and
Arduous will, ne're be in vain

For seek and search and
Be there where the eagles dare
A trek for truth in total
Solitude...a lone ranger
Combing the mountain side
A mermaid diving to the ocean floor,
In quest of a wisp of truth

Far better, the travails of hardship.
Than a bird's nest cocooned and cradled
In the midst of fallacy

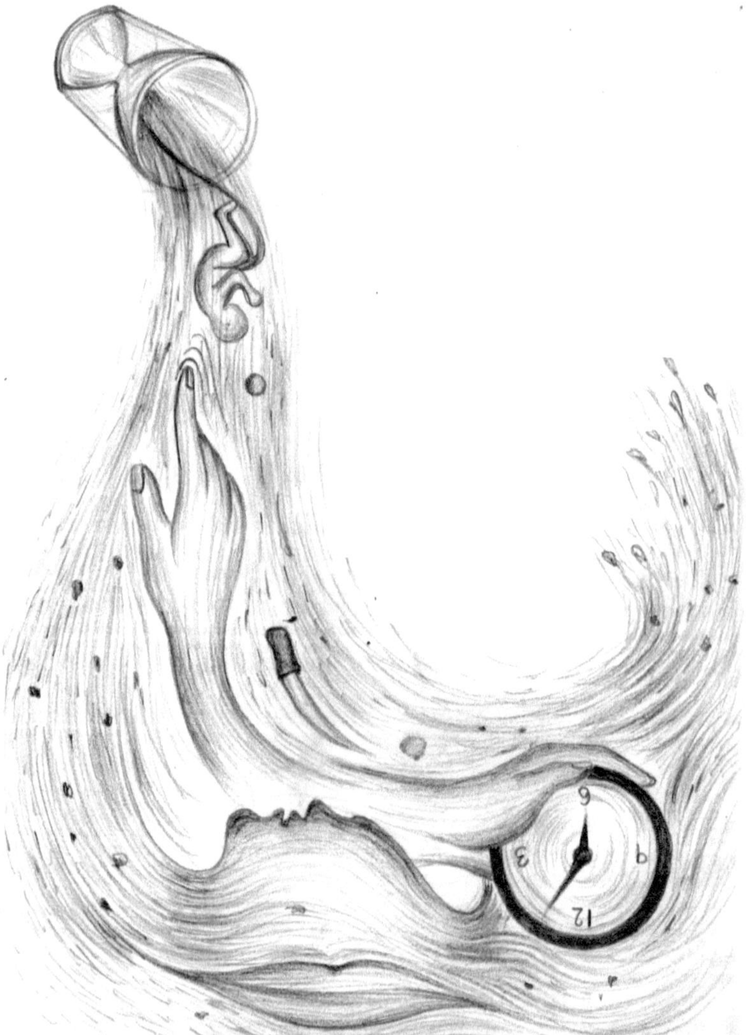

Be a leader of leaders
A damp squib for egoists
and masochists.

The Erroneous Era

Unpretentious moments so rare
Mistaken identities to care

Realities: dissect and diagnose
Selflessness, errors or humility?

A lifetime created
Or a waste of life?

An era born,
Or a foetus stilled?

Life, a perennial canal

Taking in and raking in
Imbibing the onslaught
Of cluttered and unfiltered elements
—Brimming—

A miracle may yet occur
The sluice gates may yet open
Alas!!No vent

'Tis imminent...The damn burst
Ruins of an era...or an era survived?

Time, a river
Life, moving waters
Move on, for stagnant is stagnation
Humble acceptance of errors
Humble acceptance of mistaken thoughts

Join the perennial canal
Leave the baggage
The pretentious lives

'Tis time to stake a claim
Time to break the chain
Change
For change is the only permanence
In an erroneous era!

An era of errors? Or an era fathomed?

Strength and isolation

Are strange bed-fellows!!

In Pursuit of Happiness

The tugging of heart strings,
The flow of tears,
Conjuring the fears, lurking...
Contractions and expansionAs the heart beats;
In desperation trying to conquer
The unimaginable feat.

The lowering of defences,
The deafening of senses
In search...a heart rendering
Pursuit of happiness.

The needs minimal
The search unfathomable
Deep as the ocean blue
To as far as the birds flew,
The hunger, the thirst, the search,
For the pursuit of happiness.

Just beyond the reach
of my out stretched hand,

Trembling ,quivering lips,
Just beyond the horizon
Disappearing, as a mirage,
My pursuit of happiness.

But I strode on...
An uphill tract: panting
Waiting, breathing, striding
Upwards-slowly,
Swimming against all tides,
Waves beating against my chest,
Never for an atom,
Never for a second
I thought of defeat...

I reached the shore,
I stood and embraced the skies
My pursuit had ended;
for a whileHappiness is a pursuit...unending

The will to achieve:- An analogy

It strengthens us so we may

rejoice in solitude

The Global Woman:
Wither is she Bound?

Amidst a tumultuous turbulence
Emerges the global woman,
Wither bound is she?

Unscathed from the fetters of time and tradition
Emerges a Boisterous and Brave Eve,
Wither bound is she?

From lullabies to lyrics,
From cradles to canvasses;They swim with the sharks
And play with the tadpoles-

And they exist...The road tortuous and its path be-pebbled,
The women unbridledA meandering mind...
So much to do, so much to accomplish,Wither bound is she?

They survive and they thrive
In what they do

Such is the will and such is the power
Of the global woman

Their strength lies in isolating the mind...Hither bound the global woman,
Delving into the valleys
And scaling the heights,
Going there where only the eagles dare...
Comfort crush them
And crushed comforts
Alienate them;
they adjust to live
And live to adjust...

Eloquent in their thoughts
And Napoleon in their feats :
A pregnant silence pervades
When the global womansets to conquer and defeat.

Adjustments - A reconciliation of the mind and soul. A temporary respite for a temporary remuneration

And I Walked

A boulder where the heart was
A mountain in my path....
Cross it I would...
The resolve was stout
as I stood...

Under the towering shadow,
No moonlight, no blue moon
No left over rays of twilight;
Groping ,stumbling,
Groping again.
Darkness complete within and without,
I lit a ray in the boulders;
made stouter my resolve,
Hurdles, obstacles, stones
Pebbles and boulders
Would melt under the molten lava, welling up inside
With nerves of steel...
I closed my eyes to see
Where the load led

Far ahead...I forged
As far as my nerves
Would let my eyes see

There amidst the mountains
and the vales, across the
rivers and streams;

A bright new dawn...
Engulfing the terrain
A new sun was being born
A light...
A ray...
A spark...
Of hope...lighting the fire...
I opened my eyes and the boulder was gone
The path was smooth though
Tortuous beckoning me
And I walked

A crushing of ideas and ideals

To achieve. A euphoria...

At a price.

A Painful Existence

An idealist often lives in euphoria,
A world within a world
Trusting, loving, living, longing
A fortress; a beautiful utopia!

Unaware of ill winds that blow
That would ravage the nimble mind;
Crush the humble soul...

In nature's script-less handwriting
A silent call-inaudible –
Tis, but a painful existence...

A pebble in the lake forlorn
Stripped of happiness or despair
To lie deep in the bowels
Tis but a painful existence

The utopia a mirage,
Reality, pain,
And pain...existence...

An idealist...not yet cleansed
Not sanctified furthest from our maker
Live, for pain is the spring of life—
And life
A painful existence

"Even as love crowns you

So shall the crucify you"

—Khalil Gibran

A Cotton Seed

I must have been a cotton seed,
Born to be woven and be worn
I must have been a cotton stem
To shape the yarn which shone!

Now born again, I want and yearn
The weave of the fabric I want to learn
The length and breadth
Of the warp and woof
Did I make a difference to cover the roof?

Woven and worn,
Worn and woven
Many tales told
Many weaves woven
Many fabrics sold

A yearning to become
A time weathered seed

That knows so much the weaves
Journeys taken
Miles measured
That nothing further to learn it leaves

A spec in the sky
A drop in the ocean
Need I say anymore
That every spec, that every drop
That every seed does grow
And now I am a slinky dress
Which Great Garbo wore

But once I was a cotton seed
And I am no more

SHOP
12
3
6
9

"Where you work with love you
bind yourself to yourself
and to God."

—Khalil Gibran

Alone—In the Market Place

12 months to a day ago, I stood
Where I am standing now
In the market place
A weakened soul, a heavy heart
Were thrown into my shopping cart.
A teardrop fell on my static watch
As the needles refused to move
Frozen, like lead
Weighing a ton
My limbs devoid of energy

I vowed to move the shackles of time
And charge my watch anew

The batteries charged
The moving hands...
Egged me on
and fuelled my downing spirit

So on I marched
Against the tide
An asymmetrical syndicate
Of fetters
Hindering my every move
Lugging and tugging
To push me down
A common goal it seemed

But stout I stood
As a dandelion
Ramrod straight,
Equipped for a fight
But ne've for a flight

Not reckless or impetuous,
But prudently I stood my stead
Prepared to harmonize and placate
The unseen devils and obstacles

Slowly
The syndicate disintegrated.

And formed a universal circle,
The icicles melted and hydrated
A ripple began
And then a surge,
Stagnation broke into a stream
And I snapped out of my waking dream

A stirring in my heart begins
I stand and watch
'and watch and stand
The change of time
The audible ticking

New chapters being written again
I shudder
As a teardrop falls
Damping the moving hands

Blurring my vision in the cold
I see new ones replace the old
My irises flexed
For imaged their-in
Was faith and hope
Vanquishing, desolation and despair

My shopping cart, abrim with joy
In the market place I stand
Astride my winning spirit,
Alone no more
Alone no more

A mother - A comforter of woes

A Chanakya who grows daily

And subtly.

A Twinkling Star—
A Juvenile in Jeopardy

Agile in its movement
It twinkled in mischief
Now here...
Now there...
A loner
A Juvenile in jeopardy.

Satanic forces, juxtaposed
Ambivalent, uncertain
As to the movements
Of the little star

Trying their utmost to
Ameliorate and improve their strategy

The posse of demonic forces,
Sharpening their claws
and spreading their hideous wings

To share
To capture
The twinkling star
Trying to dim its brightness

Outnumbered
But not out manoeuvred
Our little twinkling star
Endangered...alone but brave
Searching for a sign

A light shone from afar
Like a torch paving the way at par
At times brightAt times dim
Determined to reach the site
It mustered up his might
An anchor to the star
Was the light

The sojourn ended
The angles descended
And embraced
The effable star'and danced a jig
'and left the devils harem far behind

Safe and secure
The star amongst stars
At home...In the constellation
In jeopardy no more

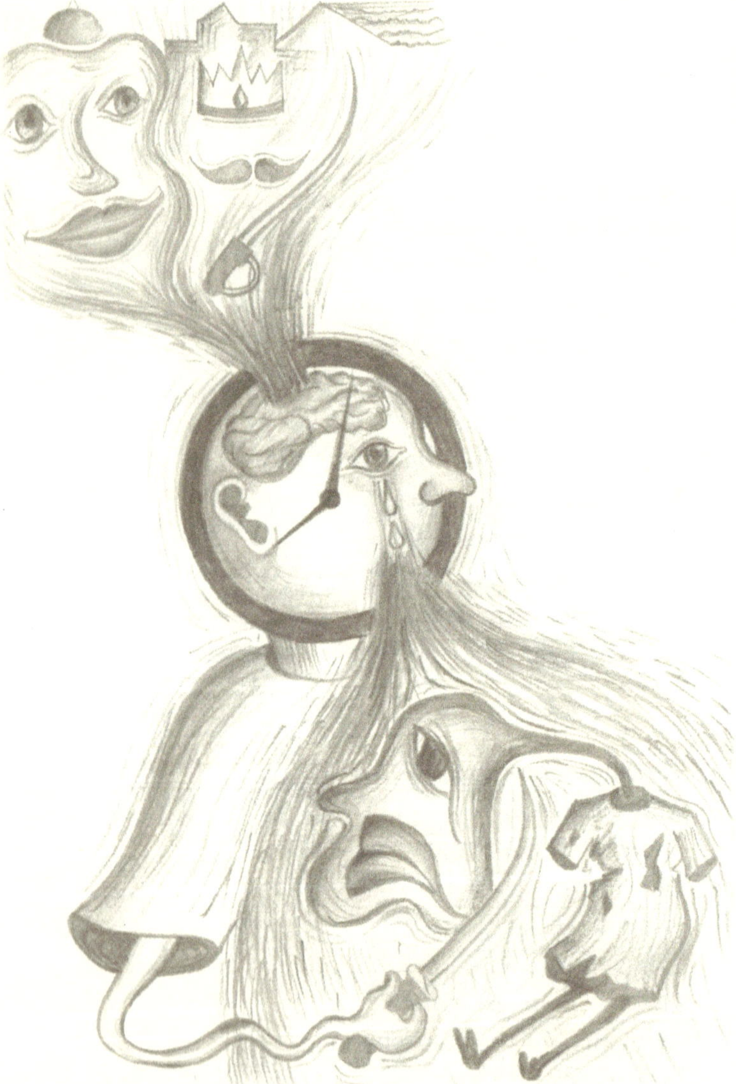

"What is Evil but the good
Tortured by its own hunger
and thirst."

—Khalil Gibran

A Silent Ode

In reminiscing mode they remain
The gurgling sounds
Like little chimes
The laughter, joy galore

For of themselves they gave
Now desolate.... yet so brave

Warrior generals of yesteryears
Now stripped of colours and of ranks
Mere soldiers they remain
Fighting for life in battle tanks...

Stooped shoulders Woeful eyes
Home alone or homeless
No shining medals to adorn
only worn out clothing
still being worn

The robust king of the treasury
Now a pathetic pauper
What fault.... what crime
For to his name, there is not a dime

The time, the grime
The blood, the sweat
No chronicles kept
No diaries written
No records of loss and gain
No records of love and pain

But Ah!! Nature has the last say
For its script-less writing
has left a silent ode

Mirrored on their countenances
The scriptures still remain
'and the laboured love was not in vain
For life goes on 'and memories short
For love and pain will spring again

Appreciation is food for the soul

When given with the Heart

not Mind

Eternity Moment

The sweet murmurings
Like silver bells from heaven
The sounds reverberating echoing
The nightingale like a pigeon
The carrier of nostalgic moments

A meeting of thoughts
Touched by the seat of all emotions
A simple moment turned to Eternity
With Voices knocking at my heart
I close my eyes and muse, was it not a most enriching experience?

A sharing of sorts
A sharing of thoughts
Ne'er for a moment
Did I falter to bear my innermost layer?
Not the dermis not the epidermis
But deep within the womb

You touched me
Where none had dared
Neither had I craved nor had cared
But you touched me

Like a lid to the eye
Breeze to the clouds
Petals to the dew
A wisp of hair to the cheeks

And now I care
For the silver bells still tingle in the air

Not a moment quiet
Not a thought free
For now a pregnant silence pervades me
A part of me you will always be
Like a simple moment turns
to eternity

Sorrow: An introduction to life

A Holiness. A consecration

A purification to anoint

our wounds.

The Awakening

Five decades of slumber
Fifty long years of sleep
Half a century of hibernation
Dawn after a dark night
Morn after the moon
The awakening

The quiet beauty spreads its rays
Engulfing the dreary darkness
Reaching even the nooks and crevices of the heart

An understanding reaching inwards
Quenching the thirst of the mind
Embracing the soul
Enlightening
A knowledge
Just grasped

Rays of hope
From futility
Joy from sorrow
A noisy peace from solitude

The beginning, a pebble
to a mountain
The path, difficult tortuous
Seemingly unattainable
A goal to nirvana
The awakening

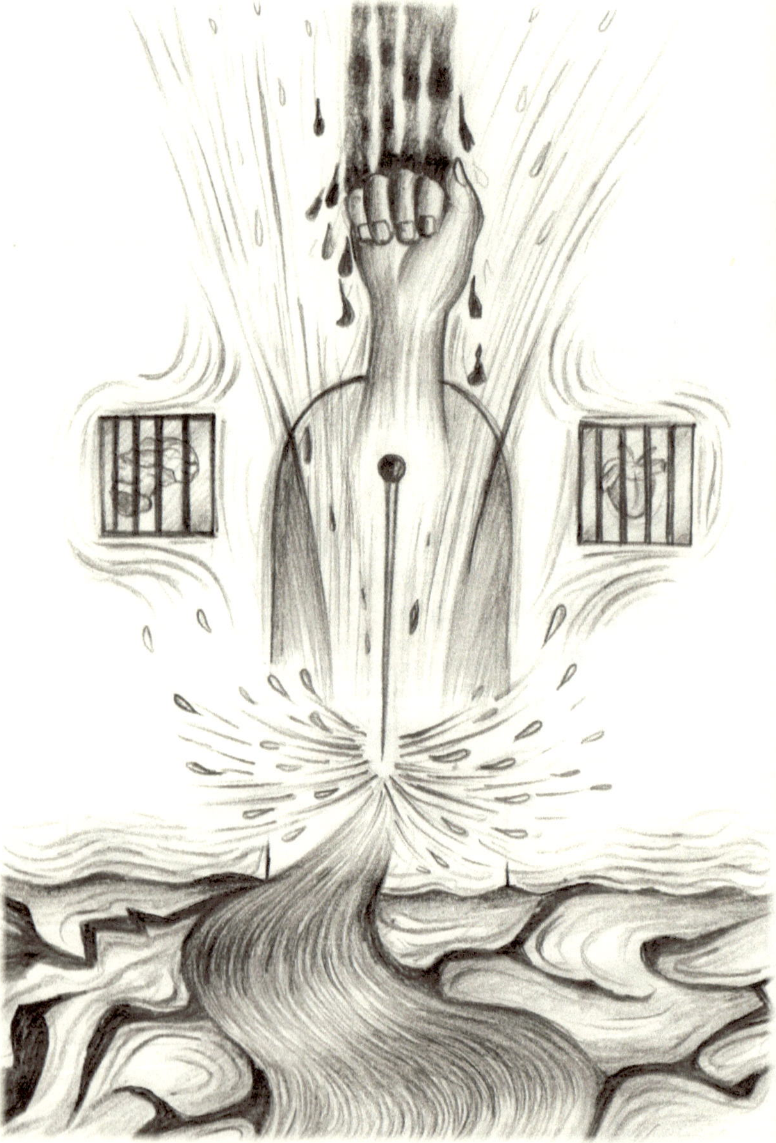

A women of substance -

An amalgamation of iron,steel

and rose petals-which spread

their fragrance yet retain

their strength

Silence

'Silence', a nameless sensitivity
An inaudible utterance
Speaking volumes, eloquently

The sound of a pin dropping
Denoting the arrival of thunder, a 'KATRINA'
No vision, no substance, no image
Nothing tangible
Just a wordless existence

No altercation, no argument, no fight
Just a soundless erosion
of sensitivity of sanity
Like an atom to a capsule of uranium
Triggering the landslide

'Silence' fills the room
Only scraping of knuckles deep sighs
No audible stirrings of the heart
or the lonely teardrops

Hoofs resounding on metalled roads
Empathising with creatures
Being smothered
Gallops bespeaking the feelings
Helplessness resigning of oneself
Trying to reach the brook

Alas! A mirage, no water
No sustenance
Just trampling of the life giving organ
Trying to resuscitate
What littlest is left, 'In Silence'

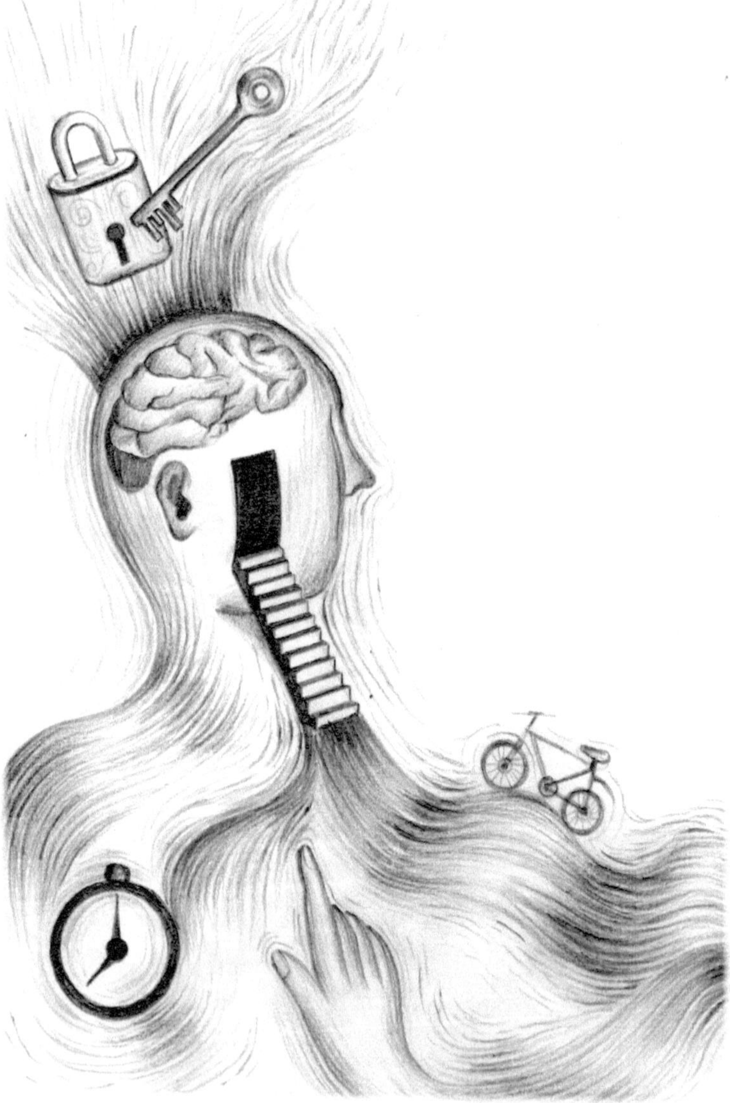

"The deeper that sorrow carves
Into your being,the more
joy you can contain."

- Khalil Gibran

Life

A journey or a trek?
An unborn foetus to the interred ashes
Or
An amalgamation of sorts
Of altruism and stoicism
Was it an empty peace
Or was it a peaceful void?

Were they ad-hoc proportions?
Or
Immaculate cocktails?
Of
Gregariousness and solitude
Of
Generosity and frugality?
A mathematical riddle
Was it a peaceful hilltop
Or was it a wasteful vale?

Life, a stupendous archaeological task
The excavations
A world of meaningless misers
Or miserably gullible philosophers

Under the mantle of magnanimity
Impervious mysteries of unseen
Of poignant reminiscing
OR
Incoherent utterances
A fine tuning
An amalgamation or dissection
A sifting or needing
a stillborn trek
OR
A fathomable journey
An empty peace
OR a peaceful void
A full circle - complete
From seed to ashes
OR
A riddle
A mystery
A quiz
Unsolved
Unresolved

Praise is prose

Heartfelt praise is poetry

Your Essence, Your Soul

Your ssence, your soul
Partners in love or matters foul
Intricate patterns woven
Intrinsic wheels driven

Your essence beckons you
Your soul awaits you
It needs no answers and asks no questions

How true is it, how pure
You are its axis
You are its fulcrum

It's leverage always favours you
Your essence, your soul
The only thing that make you whole

Enlightened spirit and ecstatic being
Condones your every act

How beatific an ally
How wonderous a being
Your essence, your soul

Your only friend in time of woe
Your armour against ill – time and foe

Your greatest warrior
Your greatest critic
Your essence, your soul.

Bask in its glory, savour its taste
Feel it's touch
Oh, how the mute senses come alive
Realisation dawns
Fragrance pervades
Realisation; your core, your being,
Fragrance, your essence, your soul.

Tears - An initiation to reality,

An anchor so we may float

and survive

When Time Stands Still

No thought of now or 'morrow
No thought of sun or moon
No thought of grandeur or riches
Nor of poverty
No thought of work or leisure
Nor of misery
When time stands still

When time stands still
The search begins

Recapturing the stolen moments
Whether a tear or a smile
Whether the agony
Or the ecstasy
The fleeting moments of truth
A mirage, lost in a transient flash
The core of sensitivity
Not a masochist, nor a stoic
When time stands still
The search begins

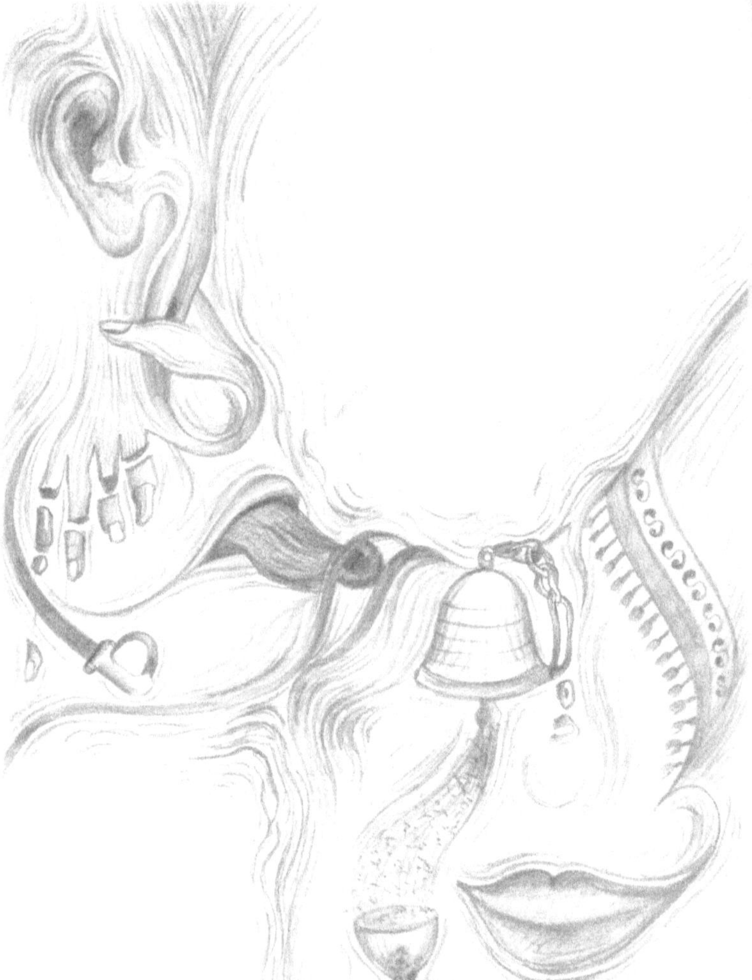

"It is well to give when asked

but it is better to give unasked,

through understanding."

- Khalil Gibran

The Lingering Cessation The Wait

The straining of ears, faint, sounds
Muscles taut, breath deepened
Heartbeats erratic

A pit for stomach
Overworked glands
Pumping of enzymes
Walls claustrophobic
Clenching and unclenching of fists
Saliva without food

The fading sounds!

The body limp, lifeless
No rhetoric
A silence sharper than a sword
Cutting across sounds

No lunar movements
Mind distraught
The magnitude of imprisonment
The cessation in sight

The breakaway, end of a term
A timeless duration...over

The jingle of bells
Harking the epilogue

Radiant countenances
Beating of drums
Sound of bugles
Laughter and tears
Ecstatic looks
Overwhelming sensitivities

A blanket of contentment
An aura of fulfilment
A beginning at the end
A nouveau experience
        A preface
        A prologue
        A new era.

आ

"You talk when you cease to be
at peace with your thoughts."

— Khalil Gibran,

The Hazy Picture

The clear cut lines of the profile
A beauty within a beauty
The sound of violin
The beat within the heart

A joyful clarity, a crystal
Merging of the souls

Disentanglement, a search,
A treasure hunt, the clues, a hazy picture

Try, plough on...in search
Of seeds sown
Harvest the crop, sift diligently
Was it a crop of grain or weeds?

Stock the grains
Rest for fodder

The chisel on the canvas
A hazy picture
With secrets buried
In her ample bosom
Mother earth looks on
Plough again
Sow and reap
Clean the hazy picture

"If you love somebody, let them go, for if they return, they were always yours. If they don't, they never were."

— Khalil Gibran

The Tumultuous Turbulence

The strife the struggle,
The storm a tornado
Furious, ravaging, destructive
Caught in its eye

The night spent in reverie
Lost in thoughts
So finely tuned

Was Gibran, in all his glory
To be accoladed?
As his words echoed –
"They come through you, not from you.
And though they are with you,
Yet they belong not to you."

Each a nucleus within itself:
Your offsprings!

Unbridled thought caused
A chaotic chaos
A tumultuous turbulence
Invaded my being

'Oh Gibran, I wish I knew...'

And suddenly as always
With an uncanny equilibrium
Peace descended and I knew

The riotous uproar
The frothing foam
The turmoil
Strange and eerie
Vanished, in a transient moment

As suddenly as it had appeared
The tumultuous turbulence
Settled and ebbed away
Like a silent psalm

A.N-
GIBRAN-(referred to the Great Khalil Gibran – The Lebanese poet

www.ingramcontent.com/pod-product-compliance
Lightning Source LLC
Chambersburg PA
CBHW022158160726
48282CB00024B/248

* 9 7 8 9 3 9 4 0 7 5 0 6 1 *